W
THE CLOUD

SALES STORIES AND ADVICE FROM

MY DAYS AT MICROSOFT

TRONG NGUYEN

WINNING THE CLOUD: SALES STORIES AND
ADVICE FROM MY DAYS AT MICROSOFT

Copyright © 2017 by Trong Nguyen

The stories in this book are all based on true events. Names, characters, organizations and situations are purposely exaggerated and liberally stretched to enhance the storytelling and illustrate key academic concepts and practical lessons learned.

For information contact: www.linkedin.com/in/megatrong

Editing by Shany Biran, Cabrina Attal, Shawn Wells and Kathy Clolinger

Cover Design and Illustrations by Pia Reyes

ISBN: 978-0-9985702-0-4

First Edition: March 2017

DEDICATION

This book would not have been possible without the support of my best friend, soulmate and life coach – Natalie Nguyen. Thank you for being the best wife any guy could have ever hoped for.

TABLE OF CONTENTS

FORWARD

The last seven years have been a trip – a rocket trip through the clouds (pun intended). I am thankful I had a chance to work for an incredible company like Microsoft and help shape the high-tech industry. We are in the nascent stages of cloud computing and it is arguably the most exciting area to be in right now.

What you are about to read are real life stories of how my team and I transformed the healthcare industry in the USA and the financial services industry in Canada. The multi-million dollar deals we signed and executed have forever changed both of these industries on a global scale.

It takes a village and an army to accomplish what we did. Selling to complex, highly-regulated, global customers is a team sport. Throughout the struggles and ultimate victories, we learned so much. I wanted to share these lessons with you in the hope that it will help you hone and sharpen your sales skills. Good selling!

CHAPTER 1

Why is She So Charismatic?

I loved Vanessa the first moment I laid eyes on her. Not the romantic kind of love but the kind of love that you reserve for special things in your life, like anything wrapped in smoked bacon or watching as your favorite sports dynasty win its sixth NBA title in Chicago.

Vanessa modeled herself after Melanie Griffith in *Working Girl*. She's got big blonde hair and that bright face and big smile that totally disarms you. She has that nasally voice and addictive accent that tells you she must have grown up in New York.

Vanessa is a contradiction wrapped up in a riddle and grounded in mid-western sensibilities. She is feminine and yet is as tough as nails. She takes her family to church every Sunday and yet she can drink 99% of the guys I know under the table. She can curse and swear with the best of them and she's not afraid to get her manicured nails dirty.

The first time I saw her do this, I laughed myself silly. We were in the midst of our territory reviews and one of the account executives was going through his client list and walking through the opportunities where he was going to grow his business for the year. Vanessa tossed her hair back, combed it with her hands and said in that nasally voice, "I don't understand." It was pretty clear that the one WHO didn't understand was the account executive because within minutes she had torn his review to shreds. Wolverine would have been impressed. And she did it all with a sparkling smile.

If you ask ten different people what makes a great leader, you would get twenty different answers. A Google search (sorry Bing!) would yield you standard answers such as, a great leader:

1. Is results oriented

2. Is customer focused

3. Has a vision

4. Is strategically focused

5. Is effective in getting work done through others

6. Is good at dealing with conflict

7. Makes high-quality decisions

8. Asks great questions

9. Is trusted

10. Is a great communicator

But do these lists really mean anything? If these qualities are tangible, wouldn't we be able to identify leaders instantaneously? Why are there such varying views on leadership? Why do so many people think Steve Jobs was a spectacular leader and you get the same amount of people that say he was the worst boss in the world? If it's so objective, why do the greatest leaders attract such polarizing views?

A few years back, I was the new account executive on a large health insurance company in the USA. Admittedly, our relationship with this client was not very good. We did not know how to work with them and they didn't know how to work with Microsoft. Culturally, we were speaking two different languages.

I arranged a dinner with Vanessa, myself and the new CTO of the insurance company. We were on a mission to cultivate and change our relationships with this important customer one step at a time. I had done my research and found out that the CTO was wicked smart, brash, and loved to provoke controversy. He would often throw ideas or thoughts out there just to see what you would say or how you would react.

"Microsoft sucks! All you guys do is PC's. You have no idea how to support an enterprise customer. All your reps know how to do is talk about licensing!" We had only just sat down, and this was how we were greeted. Our cocktails hadn't even arrived yet. Vanessa didn't miss a beat. "You guys suck too! Your operations are a mess. We can help you streamline your enterprise and cut your operational costs by at least 30% but you guys are not smart enough to listen to my team!" She went from zero to sixty faster than a Porsche 911 Turbo.

At that very moment, the waiter came with our cocktails. Vanessa took her sauvignon blanc and chugged it back.

"What else would you like to talk about?" she asked sweetly as she put down her empty wine glass.

The CTO loved Vanessa, because beyond knowing her stuff, she had charisma. It turns out, leadership and charisma are a lot like art and beauty. They are totally in the eye of the beholder. What one person finds beautiful, another person may find ugly. What one person finds charismatic, another person may find distasteful. Psychologists have found that usually a person finds someone charismatic because they are able to do things that you cannot do, or they possess talents that you do not. That's why we are innately drawn to the superstar athlete or the rock star CEO.

I was fortunate enough to go on many more sales calls with Vanessa. The more time I spent with her, the more I liked her. She had all of the characteristics of great leaders listed above, but I would tell you most leaders I know have those exact characteristics. So what made Vanessa different? What did she have that others didn't? In a word, she had authenticity. She was genuine.

Most leaders try to play the role. You always see the gloss and veneer. The general never mixes with the privates and enlisted men. That's where Vanessa was different. She was tough as nails as a boss but she was never afraid to let her guard down for you to see she was just a normal person. She had the same problems as everyone else. She had two kids that she loved but they drove her crazy sometimes. She struggled with family and work demands just like everyone else. And she wasn't so high class that she would never be seen at the local diner because it was the best value in town for breakfast. That's what made Vanessa so special. She was a superstar in every sense of the word but she was also just one of us.

Lessons Learned:

- ➢ Be very selective about who you work with. A good boss will make all the difference in the world. A good boss will help you grow, develop, and get you to where you want to go.

- ➢ If you find yourself not aligning with your boss, my recommendation is to look for other opportunities or move departments. Your boss can be mentally and emotionally draining. We spend so much time at work. Life's too short to dread work that much.

- ➢ You can't win a fight with your boss. They have positional authority and will always win in a fight.

- ➢ Middle managers are, by definition, managers. They are seldom leaders. They are there to make sure operations and the corporate machine runs smoothly. Be cautious in looking to middle managers for leadership.

- ➢ Big companies are by definition big and bureaucratic. Don't have the illusion that the top executives have it all figured out. Depending on spans and layers, sometimes they are so far removed from the day-to-day business that they make mistakes just like the rest of us.

➢ To be a leader, you need to be genuine. Listen to those who work for you and listen to what your clients say.

➢ You can be a leader at any level in the organization. When you bring value, people will look up to you, ask for your help and guidance, and seek your participation in their activities.

➢ Leadership can come in many styles. Don't have strict mental models of leadership. All leaders do not have to fit a particular profile or behave in a specific manner.

➢ When you find a leader that you respect and can learn from, embrace it and appreciate it. It is a special gift.

CHAPTER 2

I'm 6'4" and Devilishly Handsome

When you talk to sales managers or VPs of Sales, they always ask the same questions: "Do you have relationships with the CXO? What's your relationship with the CXO? How can you close that deal without the CXO's support?"

These questions are not wrong; I just don't think they're very helpful. If they just pivot a little bit, the whole conversation changes. What I would ask is, "How can we develop relationships with the CXO?" When you start asking that question, it lends itself to deeper thought and introspection.

Most sales reps take a very binary approach to relationships. On or off. They either have these relationships or they don't. At least in their minds. Invariably this perspective leads them down a linear approach to addressing the issue. If they don't have a relationship with the CXO, then they go out of their way to build that relationship directly. They invite the CXO to social events, dinners, and whatever else they can in the hopes that these bonding moments will lead to future sales.

Direct strategies are useful in certain situations, but not all of them. I would submit that there may be a better way to build these executive relationships. Instead of going at it head on, I want to provide you with a framework in which to think about how you can develop and influence your relationships. This framework is applicable in your personal life as well as your business life. It's applicable whether you are a customer-facing sales representative or if your work function is internal facing.

In the 1960s, industrial psychologists David Merrill and Roger Reid did an extensive study around dimensions of assertiveness and responsiveness. From that study, they came up with a 2x2 matrix outlining four social styles:

analytical, driving, expressive, and amiable. When I first read the study, I wept for days. I was overcome with joy. Forget SpaceX or Tesla, this revelation was akin to Elon Musk harnessing his brilliance in physics and engineering to find a way to create hickory smoked bacon out of thin air.

Here's the practical application of this theory:

1. **Step 1:** Perform a personality analysis on the CXO, senior executive, or any person you want to build a relationship with and place them in one of the four quadrants.

2. **Step 2:** Then, look at all of the people that influence that person. Do a personality analysis on those people and place them into the appropriate quadrants.

3. **Step 3:** Now think about all of the people that influence the people that influence the client. Do a personality analysis on those people and place them into the right quadrants.

4. **Step 4:** Complete a relationship alignment exercise. Find the right people in your organization to connect to all of those people you have identified and start building those relationships.

Here is the execution of the process in visual form.

Merrill-Reid Personality Analysis

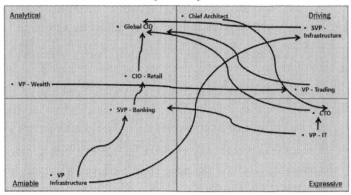

Over time, what you have essentially done is executed a complete surround strategy. The main reason why this strategy works is because you are not dependent on one person for success or failure. In our highly matrixed world, decisions are made by committees or groups of people. That's why this strategy has been so successful.

I was working with a global manufacturing company based in Chicago and executed this strategy to build the right relationships with the Global CIO. Along the way, I had built relationships with the VP of Architecture, SVP of Operations, SVP of Infrastructure, etc. It took me six months and I hadn't spent any time with the Global CIO at all. Instead of shooting for the moon right away, I first built a ladder to the clouds.

By now I had solved numerous complex issues for this company and had built up my brand as a creative problem solver and Mr. Fixit. It didn't matter if you had hardware issues, software issues, etc. With some duct tape, vinegar and a pair of chopsticks, I could make MacGyver look bad. I completely influenced those who would influence the Global CIO.

With reputation in hand, I asked the Chief Technology Officer to introduce me to the Global CIO. When I went into the meeting, she said something to me that I will never forget. She said, "Trong, after all of the great stories I had heard about you, I just pictured you would be 6'4" and devilishly handsome."

I told her I was! It was the start of an enduring and beneficial relationship.

Lessons Learned:

➢ Developing senior executive relationships takes time. Focus on strategies that develop these long-term relationships. Like all relationships, trust is earned, and it is earned over time.

➢ If an executive tells you how powerful they are in the company, they aren't. The only ones that tell you that are the insecure ones who aren't the real decision makers. Einstein didn't have to go around telling people how smart he was. You just knew.

➢ Be genuine and authentic. Smart people will see right through people who aren't genuine. If you don't like sports, don't pretend to be a sports fan just to impress a customer. Find some other common ground to build the relationship on.

➢ Influence those who would influence the relationships you want to develop.

➢ Do a personality analysis to understand the person you want to develop a relationship with so that you understand their motivations and what makes them tick.

➢ Use multiple approaches for building relationships. These include direct, indirect, and surround strategies.

➢ Focus on adding value, as that will be the foundation for long-term relationships.

➢ Network and build relationships well before you need them. When the time comes, they will be more open to helping you.

➢ Integrity is a non-negotiable. Work only with people of integrity. Stay clear of those who are morally ambiguous.

➢ Leadership styles and approaches change over time. A leader who was good in a particular time and situation may not be suited for others.

Trong Nguyen

CHAPTER 3

I Pity the Fool

When I started my sales career, I had the best mentor. His name was Claude. Everyone loved Claude. He was a big cuddly teddy bear of a man who was as strong as he was caring. He was always the life of the party and magnetic like the North Pole. You know the type. Someone who is larger than life even when he's standing right in front of you.

Claude didn't teach me how to build executive relationships or close multi-million dollar deals. He didn't teach me how to negotiate with a six-year-old (really hard) or distort reality the way Steve Jobs did (even harder). He taught me something much more important. He taught me how to be nice.

I followed Claude around for a year just carrying his bag. I was happy to carry his bag. I wanted to carry his bag. I dissected his every move with scientific precision the way Benedict Cumberbatch dissects the truth on *Sherlock*. After a couple of months, I was completely baffled. I knew the numbers didn't lie because I had been witness to it.

Claude spent 40% of his time with customer managers and executives. He spent another 30% of his time with the executive assistants (EAs) and technical engineers from our customers. The remaining 30% of his time he spent with the administrative assistants and technical engineers on our team.

What was confusing about this – at least to me – was how Claude was the ultimate closer. When you needed to land some whales or elephants, you sent in Claude. If Claude had been a Navy Seal, I'm convinced we would have found Osama Bin Laden years earlier. He was that good.

Seeing Claude in action was like watching Michelangelo paint the Sistine Chapel. He knew every executive assistant's history, their background, what they liked and all about their families. When it was a special event like Christmas, he would never take the executives out. He would always take out the EAs and made sure they had the time of their lives. He brought them little pieces of chocolate here and there just to let them know he was thinking about them.

I asked Claude one day why he spent so much time with the EAs and technical engineers. The answer was suspiciously cryptic. Claude said, "Dude, you should watch *The A-Team!*" I had no idea what he was talking about but I watched that show religiously. A special-ops team, going around doing good for people while they hid from the government. I didn't see the relevance. For the longest time, I thought Claude just wanted me to go around blowing things up or at a minimum smoke a cigar the way Hannibal did.

I've had the chance to work with some talented executive assistants. At the highest levels, the EAs work so closely with the senior executive that they become their work spouses. They understand every nuance of the executive, what their preferences are, and how they would react to things.

Years and decades later I have never forgotten this lesson from my Sensei. I love watching sales reps while they are waiting for their CXO meeting. Are they nice to the receptionist? Are they nice to the EA? Are they so full of themselves that they think they are more important than anyone else?

It's exactly like people watching in New York City. You'd be shocked at what you see. You see people from all walks of life. You see extremely rich people and you see lots of folks that just need a bit of help. It is always interesting to see how some of the rich people treat the poorer people. When I see these things, I'm reminded of that famous quote from Mr. T in his most famous role on *The A-Team*, "I pity the fool!" How we treat others always has a way of ricocheting back to us.

I worked with a top-notch executive assistant at a global financial services company and, truth be told, she was better than most of the VPs that I have worked with. Colleen was smart, witty and funny. She had all the IQ but more importantly she had Emotional Quotient. Whenever I needed to deliver a tough message to the Global CIO or was stuck in a critical stage of a deal, I always used Colleen as a sounding board. Like bourbon-dipped, honey-glazed, bacon-wrapped shrimp, I was never disappointed. She always gave me the best advice. This is the value that Claude saw in the low-level workers of any company. They were the ones who got things done and kept things moving. They were the important ones.

Are you valuing the real people that make a difference? Or are you the fool?

Lessons Learned:

➤ For the top-level executive, their executive assistant is usually their right-hand person. Treat them like gold.

➤ The executive assistants and the operations staff are usually the most important people on the team. They help you get access to the executives, know how their companies operate, and have all the tribal knowledge to get things done.

➤ Always get the receptionists, executive assistants, and operational staff of your customers the occasional treat. They will appreciate that you have been thoughtful and it will pay you back in spades.

➤ Don't forget Administrative Professionals Day. It is one of the most important days of the year.

➤ For special events like Christmas, take out the executive assistants and operations staff for lunch. They appreciate it so much more. The normal sales rep always takes out the executives or middle managers. Don't be a normal sales rep. This is your chance to stand out from the pack.

CHAPTER 4

Why Lunch Doesn't Matter

I want to tell you a story. Like all good stories, you have to read between the lines to see what is really going on. But the verses and the refrain of this particular story can be universally applied to all of us. It's not just my story, in other words; it's everybody's. I had been asked to join Microsoft as a sale rep to tackle one of their toughest customers. This customer was highly decentralized and scattered throughout the USA. They had their own unique culture and Microsoft had burned through account managers every year with the hope that someone would be able to find the secret to cracking this customer. On the surface this customer seemed irrational, overly demanding, and completely wrapped up in their own little bubble. They didn't like the way we did things. Didn't they know who we were? We are Microsoft! Everyone wants to buy our stuff...

Right?

In a short period of time I was able to turn around the relationships. It's all in the approach, as it turns out, and I had the right one. I became a trusted advisor with most of the C-Suite. The CFO, COO, CMO and senior executives always took my meetings. These relationships helped us build the bridge that was needed to make this customer a vanguard in its industry. They were one of the first customers in a highly-regulated industry to go to the cloud. For instance, Office 365 enabled them to become highly agile, effectively integrating their many disparate acquisitions, and truly enabling employee collaboration.

Back at Microsoft, we were on cloud nine (no pun intended). We had cracked the code and were able to get one of our toughest customers to embrace us and the future – cloud computing. Like most great process and analytics companies, we started doing some forensics, deal reviews, and analysis to see how we could cookie cutter this alchemy onto other businesses and make this same win for them as well. Could I repeat the magic? That was the question.

When they went through my time and expense reports for the previous two-year period, they hit the jackpot. Ding Ding Ding! We have the answer! Our analysts found out that for the most part, every breakfast, lunch and dinner I'd had over that two-year period were with customers. There was a complete correlation. You have meals with your customers to build relationships. These relationships help build trust. Once you build trust, then you can close massive deals to achieve quota. Wash, rinse, repeat. The answer was so plain and obvious, we had to wonder why we didn't see it before.

When the analysis was revealed, I chuckled a bit. It made me think about a statistics professor I had in university. At the beginning of every class he said, "There are lies, damned lies, and then there are statistics!" This little saying always stuck with me. It rings as true today as it did 110 years ago, when Mark Twain first said it. The missing insight from the company's analysis was, "Why did Trong have so many of his meals with his customer?" If they had asked that question, they would have found out the real reason, for it was simple. The customer and I were so busy that this was the only time we could meet. The customer was busy working on key initiatives to help transform their company, and I was busy helping with various initiatives that would enable the customer to execute that transformation. We had common and shared goals. Eventually, as with all busy people, we had to eat at some point. We used those mealtimes to catch up and stay in sync and ensure that our projects were aligned.

When most new sales reps are out meeting with customers, one of the first things they invariably say is, "We should grab lunch…" I cringe every time I hear it because it is so cliché. Neither side means it. Plus, the customer automatically starts to mentally paint the picture of a typical sales rep who adds no value but can buy them a free meal.

At a minimum, it takes two hours to have lunch with a customer. Yes, that long! It's a minimum of 30 minutes to prepare for it. You have to do your background research. At least 30 minutes for traveling. And then at a minimum it is 60 minutes for lunch. That's a quarter of your workday. And that is assuming you don't have a "Don Draper" *Mad Men* lunch. Everyone is really busy. In our 24/7 world, could our time be better used?

Breakfast is the most important meal of the day. But – and hear me out – I would argue that you can miss lunch. You'll be further ahead. The foundation of any meaningful and long-term relationship is shared experiences and shared goals. If the sales rep took those two hours that would have been spent on lunch and, instead, focused deeply on adding value to the customer and helping to solve the problems that their customers are working on, then that would become the foundation for their relationship. Now there are shared and common goals that can act as a bridge to building the desired relationships. It's not about drinks or a fancy meal. Not about having a steak and a glass of wine, no matter how enjoyable that might be. That wasn't the point of my lunches. The point was to add value for the customer in the only time we had.

The next time you are out on a sales call and are coaching a new sales rep, watch for the cues. Do they automatically jump to drinks, lunch or dinner to build rapport or a relationship? Or do they go back to first principles to see what the issues and problems are and see how their solutions can help solve these customer problems?

What do you think? Does lunch really matter?

Lessons Learned:

➤ Focus on adding value to your customers. That is the north star that will lead you to building great customer relationships and closing deals.

➤ Relationships are built on shared and common goals. Find out what those goals are with your customers. Use those as the bridge to building long-term relationships.

➤ Some social activities can be used to jumpstart relationships but long-term meaningful relationships develop through adding value and building trust. The social activities will naturally develop as a result of building that trust.

➤ Let your customers decide where to eat and what social activities to do. As sales reps, we do this every day so it is not a big deal to us. For most customers, it is a treat for them to have that occasional lunch or dinner out. So let them decide the venue.

➤ Be wary of metrics and data that big companies compile. Taken out of context, they never truly tell the whole story. Metrics and data (like my T&E reports) can always be twisted to tell the story you want to tell.

➢ The general perception is that most sales reps are only good for paying for lunch and drinks. Don't fall into that stereotype. Focus on the work and the value. You will be so busy with your customer that meals and drinks will naturally flow as you start to bond through shared and common goals.

➢ When you are going through RFP stages or blackout periods, make sure you obey the rules. You don't want to inadvertently put your clients at risk by taking them out to lunch or dinner when you were not supposed to.

➢ When you are out with your clients, don't be afraid to let your guard down. Tell them about your family and personal life. The more that they see you as a person, the easier it will be for you to connect on an emotional level.

➢ At some point, your clients will ask you to connect with them on social media such as Facebook or Instagram. My recommendation is to do it! They trust and like you enough to open up their world to you – accept it and reciprocate.

Trong Nguyen

CHAPTER 5

Boys Don't Cry

I have a confession to make. I used to cry. I used to cry every time *Glengarry Glen Ross* ended. And I watched it 482 times. If God had made a movie, this would have been it. School taught me how to crunch numbers but I learned my ABCs at the altar of Glengarry.

Every profession has that safe place that they call home. The place where they go to hone their craft. Doctors have medical schools. Actors have theater groups. Sales reps, on the other hand, can learn everything they need to know by mimicking and practicing the slick sales moves perfected by Al Pacino, Jack Lemmon and Alec Baldwin in this unforgettable movie.

In sales, the running joke is that it never pays to be honest. Most sales reps love *Wall Street* and *Boiler Room* the way they love their mothers. We wanted to be the bond traders in Liar's Poker and we cried when Tom Cruise said, "Show me the money!" We cried not because it was a great love story or because the protagonist had such altruistic goals. No. We cried because Jerry was dumb enough to be honest about it.

In typical Hollywood fashion the hero triumphs, and what we're left with is an empty feeling. Does it really work that way? Does it pay to be honest? That's the question these movies put to us. For the longest time, I thought the answer was no.

There are a couple of prevailing theories in honesty research. Moral philosophers and cognitive psychologists have had long-standing, contrasting hypotheses about the mechanisms governing the tradeoff between honesty and self-interest.

The "Grace" hypothesis suggests that people are innately honest and have to control honest impulses if they want to profit. The "Will" hypothesis holds that self-interest is our automatic response.

There is probably some truth to the stereotypes that customers have regarding sales reps. The perception is that most sales reps are only interested in maxing out their commissions and then moving on as quickly as possible before the customer finds out the truth. Sales reps want to make the most money possible and are willing to do whatever it takes to get a deal done. So goes the stereotype.

I get asked a lot about how I am able to consistently close game-changing multi-million dollar deals that no one else could. The answer usually surprises everyone. I just tell them that I'm completely transparent and honest with the CXOs. I tell them the good, the bad, and the ugly whether they want to hear it or not. I tell them the truth.

One of the first times that I met with the CFO of a global pharmaceutical company, he asked me what was wrong with the company. I told him nothing was wrong with the company but rather his mergers and acquisitions strategy was flawed. He was taken aback that a high-tech sales rep would question his finance skills and strategy. When I explained to him the rationale, he completely got it. From that point on, he became my sponsor in the company.

Most sales reps, when they meet a senior executive from their customers for the first time, are hesitant to be honest and open in their conversations. They start to sugarcoat things which invariably leads to a diluted message. What they don't realize is that this happens everywhere. The sales rep would stand out more if he was completely honest.

In McKinsey's breakthrough work on spans and controls, it was determined that the best-run organizations have six to seven layers from the lowest level employee to the CEO. So you can imagine what happens in an organization. At the lowest level, there may be a problem, and that problem gets reported up the chain of command. By the time, it gets to the CIO, CFO, or CEO there is absolutely no problem. Too many filters exist between the bottom and the top.

When I sit with the CXOs at my customer businesses, I always preface by saying that I know this is none of my business because it is their company. I then begin to outline what I think the issue is. I always end by telling them not to take my word for it but to check with the following people in their organization.

Three things always happen. First, the CXO is surprised by what I just told him/her because of the filtering effect. Second, they always go and check. Third, they always find an issue! Bingo! Honesty works and stands out because at their levels, everyone is scared to be honest with them. This is when trust gets built and relationships start to form. This is how I get my second and third meetings with senior executives.

I have a confession to make. I used to cry, but I laugh a lot now. I laugh at all the things that I use to idolize and worship. I laugh because I realize how naïve and misguided I was. The art and craft of sales (and it is a craft) is so different from what we see or think it is.

When you have a quiet moment, ask yourself. Do you laugh? Or do you cry? Or do you maybe do a little bit of both?

Here's an example of a 1-pager that I use when I go into my executive meetings.

Karen Johnson (Global CIO)   05/10/2016

Item	Comments	Status
Executive Briefing	• Review Agenda • Dinner Plans – Steak or Seafood?	
Cloud	• Contracts – progressing slowly. • Projects – under way	
Operations	• Chile • Colombia • Mexico	
None of My Business	• Infrastructure Teams – Not supporting initiatives • Finance Teams – Not adding value • **Peter Jones** – Advocating DB2 database over Microsoft SQL. Why? • **Joe Smith** – Really weak SVP. I call him the $10M man because that's what he is costing the company in lost savings. • **Chris Rodriguez** - Advocating private cloud over public cloud. Subverting our progress. • **Joe Jackson** – He needs to get a new job! He's too good for what he is doing now!	
All Other Business	• What else did you want to cover?	

Lessons Learned:

➢ When dealing with your client senior executives, the best rule of thumb is to be honest. Rarely do they get sales reps who will tell them what is truly going on at the lower levels. Remember the lesson on spans and controls.

➢ Executives at the highest levels (whether at the customer or in your own company) can't fix the problems unless they know what they are. So much information gets filtered before it gets to them that it is hard for them to truly know the root or depth of a problem.

➢ When providing facts and data to senior executives, make sure you triple and quadruple check your facts to support your positions. Providing inaccurate facts will kill any good will or reputation you might have previously established. Be very judicious in using this approach.

➢ Credibility takes time to develop. Little baby steps will lead to bigger steps that will lead to developing solid relationships with customers.

➢ Tell your customers not to trust or believe you. It is in their best interest to check and validate what you are saying. Senior executives always validate controversial statements or issues so you should be prepared for them to look into what you have said.

➢ Be prepared for the fallout and flack at the middle management level when you start escalating. At this point, you need to make a determination of whether or not the ends justify the means. Are you willing to live with the repercussions of stirring the pot?

➢ When you go into tough customer situations, make sure you prepare your team and executive leaders so that they understand the approach and game plan. This ensures that you don't step on each other's toes in the meeting.

➢ In certain situations and circumstances, you may find that you were completely wrong. The best approach here is to be honest about it. Tell your clients where and why you were wrong. They will appreciate and respect the candor.

CHAPTER 6

Nature vs. Nurture

Nature or nurture? This question was first framed by Francis Galton in 1883 and debates have raged ever since. It has incited such polarizing views because if we are ever able to answer that question, the practical implications would be invaluable to every area of society. We would be able to raise and foster a new generation of leaders, athletes, and superstars in every field conceivable.

At Microsoft, we would answer questions like, "Why can't we increase our revenues? What are the indicators for who will make the best sales people? Are the best sales reps made or born? Should you hire introverts or extroverts? Is sales just a God-given gift or is there an ideal way to nurture talent?" These questions are a top priority for most CEOs and VPs of Sales in every organization.

A few years ago, I joined Microsoft in Chicago and was as green as an edamame bean. People say that IBM is the mother of matrixed organizations, and they would be completely right. Microsoft, however would definitely rank a very close second. Microsoft had a direct sales teams, overlay sales teams, overlay on top of the overlay sales teams, marketing teams and overlay on the marketing teams. This structure was replicated across every function. Garmin's GPS products have helped a billion people find their way through dense metropolises the world over, but they could never make a device to navigate Microsoft's innards.

On arrival at the maze that is Microsoft, I instantly recognized that I needed a mentor, and I needed someone really good. Selling to customers I could do, that was easy. However, if I couldn't navigate Microsoft itself, it really didn't matter. I would be completely ineffective as an advocate for my customers if I couldn't figure out how to get things done internally. If I was ineffective for my customers, then I might as well find another job.

I asked around and there was one universal answer: "You need to talk to Dave." Everyone I asked had a 'Dave story' and when they were done telling their story, I would invariably laugh myself silly. They were just so funny. From these stories, I gathered that Dave was **THE** closer. He only hunted whales and he made more money than any one person could spend in a lifetime. I doubted that the stories were true, but if nothing else, they were good for a chuckle.

One of the first stories that I heard about Dave revealed something important about how he acted and thought. Dave and a new sales specialist on his team were going to meet near the customer's office, prepare, and then head to the meeting together. The sales specialist drove up in a beat-up jalopy and dressed too casually.

As the story goes, words were exchanged. Actually, there was no exchange. It was all one way. Dave told the new sales specialist, "Take some f*cking pride in yourself. We work for a market leader. They pay you really well. Go get a f*cking nice car and some nice clothes. And don't come back until you do! Have some pride!"

With that, he dismissed the sales specialist and went on the sales call by himself. The guys at the office laughed for months after that. That was typical Dave. We might all have thought what he was thinking in that situation, but he had the gonads to actually say it.

The first time I met Dave, he came as advertised. Draped in his Armani suit and laced in Ferragamos, he slowly eased out of his Mercedes S65 AMG. I asked him how his weekend was and he said "It was f*cking shit!" He had blown two motors racing his speedboat. They cost $50K a pop. Of course! What else would Dave be doing on the weekend?!

I walked Dave through my customer situation and explained the struggles I was having getting everyone internally aligned and heading in the same direction so that we could all be effective and successful. I sat there like a sophomore in high school. I was enamored with my teacher and taking enough notes to fill three spiral binders. Dave provided such clarity of thought. I savored the moment the way you romance your first sip of coffee in the morning, or your first Tanqueray and Tonic in the afternoon.

I got my graduate degree from The University of Chicago but I was definitely going to get my PhD from *The University of Dave.* From that point on, every time I had a tough problem to think through, I called Dave. It was like having Sonny Crockett as my personal mentor. He taught me it was OK to blow things up to get the job done. He taught me that if you wanted results, sometimes you have to make people or situations uncomfortable. That's how you move inertia and status quo in the right direction. Dave asked me a pointed question one time that has stuck with me ever since, "Do you want to make the news or do you want to report the news?" That got to the essence of why he was so successful.

Throughout my freshman year at Microsoft I called Dave every week. He coached and mentored me on how to get my first big deal done for the cloud. Dave helped me lay booby traps and land mines that would blow up all of the customer's objections and get the ball moving to help transform their business.

So are leaders made or are they born? There seems to be a consensus forming over the last few years that it's a bit of both and I think this is the right perspective. We are all born with some innate characteristics (IQ, physical attributes, introversion/extroversion) but other attributes such as passion, drive, self-belief, and emotional intelligence can be shaped by our environment. One of the best ways we can control our shaping is to choose mentors who foster the development of our best selves. I am thankful I was born with certain traits and attributes. However, I'm more thankful for people like Dave and other mentors I've found along the way who helped nurture me. Without their coaching, mentorship, and guidance, I would never have become the seller that I am today.

Lessons Learned:

- ➢ Seek out people who are the best at what they do and ask them to be your mentors. They have been there and done it. They can teach you how to get to where you want to go faster. The mentor/protégé relationship is a lifelong one.

- ➢ Do you want to make the news or report the news? That will dictate how you will act and behave. Some people like to be on the sidelines and watch things happen. Some people like to be the ones that make things happen. Figure out which one of those people you are.

- ➢ Don't be afraid to be outlandish or controversial. It will get you the attention you need to make a difference. People always remember the peacock.

- ➢ You have to have a core set of characteristics but you can definitely be shaped and molded to be the next generation of leaders. Superstars are made, not born.

- ➢ Give back. At some point, people will seek you out to be their mentors. Be judicious on who you select and how you spend your time, but it is always beneficial to assist others.

Trong Nguyen

CHAPTER 7

What are you Scared of?

It's fascinating that as a kid everything seems so much bigger than it really is. Your dad seems to be this Goliath that could squash the Hulk with his pinky. The snow banks around the neighborhood look like they could dwarf Mt. Everest or at least Mt. Rainer.

As adults, not much really changes. We usually make a bigger deal out of things than they really are. Our highs are really high and our lows are really low. In the corporate world, we especially apply this optic when it comes to hierarchy.

Heuristics is the study of human decision making that was first developed by Israeli psychologists Amos Tversky and Daniel Kahneman. Simply put, it is how we use experience and practical shortcuts to solve complex problems. This helps us get immediate answers when long cognitive processing to find the best solution is impossible or impractical.

In sales, we consciously use this methodology every day to influence our customers. Whether it is the anchoring, familiarity, or escalation of commitment heuristic, we use it to our advantage to further the sales process.

What happens though when we don't recognize that we are unconsciously applying a heuristic to our professional or personal life? How much of a disadvantage are we at? I would submit to you that it is quite a bit.

Sometimes we inadvertently use positional authority or hierarchy as a heuristic on ourselves. When we meet the CXO or President of a company, we immediately think that they must be special or they are graced with some magical talent that we are not blessed with.

I was like Russell Crowe in *Gladiator*. Completely unstoppable. If you wanted to close the game changing deals, if you wanted to blow out the numbers, if you wanted to overthrow empires, you called me. I was the closer.

And then I went home. I would run the house like I run my business at work. I was shouting out orders quicker than *Rain Man* could count numbers or match sticks. God, it felt good. I had arrived. And then reality hit. In under a minute my wife and three kids put me in my place.

They didn't care what I did at work, what kind of multi-million dollar deals I had just closed or how much money we just made. All they knew was that I was their dad and I was there to help them with homework, change their diapers and cook my sinfully delicious pancakes on-demand.

It would be years later until I began to appreciate what I really had at home. I had a mechanism that grounded me and brought me back to earth. No matter how big my head or ego got, I was reminded when I got home that I was as normal as everyone else.

Bill Gates was once asked in an interview, "You are the richest and most powerful man in the world. What's your life like at home? Do your kids obey your every command?" Bill said, "Kids are kids. My kids don't know who Bill Gates is, they just know that I am their dad."

I get asked a lot by new sales reps, "Trong, how do you spend time with all of these senior executives and how do you build such symbiotic relationships? How do I get to that level of excellence?" The answer usually surprises them.

I tell them that the senior execs that we work with are just normal people. They have the same problems that we all have. This answer usually surprises them. The new sales reps think that there is some magic or voodoo I must be conjuring to get the results that I get.

To prove my point, I invite senior executives from our customers into our account planning sessions. When they are there, I do an hour Q&A session with these executives. I probe with a lot of personal questions. Where were they born? Where did they live? I ask about their families, where they went to school, etc.

By the time we are done, my team is usually floored. I've just taken one of the top executives that we work with as our customers and made them human. They have the same home issues that we have. They help with homework, change diapers, and are secretly scared of their wives as well!

Here's an example of the questions I ask on a cue card.

Jane Smith – Global CIO Questions

1. Where were you born? How many brothers and sisters do you have?
2. Where did you go to school?
3. Did you consider careers other than banking?
4. What do you like to do in your spare time? What do you like to do for fun?
5. What's your greatest strength? What do you need to improve on?
6. If you could change one thing about you, what would it be?
7. Name a vendor or partner that you think really highly of. Why?
8. What's the most difficult part of the job? What's the most fun part about the job?
9. You've spent a lot of time in different parts of the business, how has this helped you prepare for your current role?
10. Who are some leaders you look to? Why?
11. Looking back on your career, would you have done anything differently?
12. If money were not an issue and you could do anything you want as a profession, what would you do?

The next time you are out with a senior executive and are nervous because of their title and position, just remember that they are like everyone else. We are all just people. When you come from that perspective, everything else will fall into place.

Lessons Learned:

> CXOs and top executives are just normal people. Don't be scared of them. They have the same issues and problems as the rest of us. They put on their pants one leg at a time just like the rest of us.

> Inviting top executives to meet and talk to your team will humanize them and provide you with a different perspective. It gives the executive a chance to meet and understand the motivations behind your team. It gives your team a chance to understand what makes the executive tick.

> Beware of biases and heuristics such as positional authority as they will alter how you should behave. Read works from the godfathers of human psychology and decision making – Amos Tversky and Daniel Kahneman.

> Find creative and fun ways to integrate customer executives into your planning and business development sessions. They will provide more insight than if you just had an internal meeting.

> Let your team help shape the agenda and the format of your account planning sessions. This ensures that they get what they need out of the session.

> Bring your executives and leadership team to the account planning session. They need to be an integral part of your business.

> When customers are part of the process, they feel more vested in making you successful as well. They now have stake in the game.

> Read Michael Lewis' new book <u>The Undoing Project: A Friendship That Changed Our Minds</u>. It is a great book that delves into the origins of heuristics and how Amos Tversky and Daniel Kahneman shaped how we think.

Trong Nguyen

CHAPTER 8

What's for Breakfast?

Satya Nadella, Microsoft's CEO, is obsessed with changing and shaping Microsoft's culture. Satya says that a company is nothing more than a collection of its people and that culture is nothing more than the collective expression of these people. Therefore, all the people in a company get to effectively shape the culture through their individual actions, behaviors, and judgments.

At a macro level, we intuitively know that Satya is right about the importance of culture. Many of us have had front row seats to some of the biggest failed mergers and acquisitions in the 1980s and 1990s. You name an industry and we can come up with failed mergers caused by culture. We saw it with Daimler/Chrysler, Novell/WordPerfect, and Sprint/Nextel. The list is long.

Early in my career I got to work with an industry icon called Digital Equipment Corporation (DEC). The people were unforgettable and the culture was even better. Most people compared the culture of DEC to that of Microsoft in the early days.

DEC was a sinking ship and everyone inside was happy to go down with it. That's how absorbing the culture was. Then Compaq bought DEC. The cultures of the two companies were so different that you could see sharks circling around prey before the ink was dry on the legal contracts. That was the beginning of the end for Compaq.

So clearly culture is an important consideration during big mergers, but is Peter Drucker right when he says culture eats strategy for breakfast? And does it apply at the micro level context of a sales team going in to work with a customer? Is culture even relevant and should you care about it?

I experienced the importance of culture firsthand while working on a very challenging project with a global pharmaceutical company in 2010. I had watched a bunch of our sales reps parade in and out of this company. All of these sales reps were top notch in our company. They were bright, seasoned and all came to the table with their "A" game.

They did regression analyses and compiled strategic frameworks that would make Michael Porter dizzy. They built relationship alignment strategies, heat maps, white space analyses... Heck, they even figured out how Matt Damon could survive on Mars for <u>eight</u> years! Yet they all failed. The customer didn't embrace them and eventually they all left the account.

I started spending time with this customer, doing all the traditional sales rep stuff. I knew all of their financials and how we could help reduce operational costs or drive revenue growth using Microsoft technologies. I started to build the right relationships at the highest levels. And yet I felt that something was missing. I hadn't touched their soul; I didn't get the essence of what they were about yet. I was neglecting their culture.

Logan was a manager on their architecture team. If you were to look up the definition in the dictionary of good people or the salt of the earth, Logan's picture would be right there. Logan was one of those people that everyone loved. He dove into teamwork, always saw the cup as half full and embraced you with a southern hospitality from a bygone era.

One day Logan and I were talking about our families. Logan told me about his family and why he was in Florida working remotely instead of the northeast with the rest of his team and company. It turned out Logan's son had a special medical condition and they figured out that Florida, with its unique weather and humidity, was the perfect climate and environment for his son. My heart broke because I could visualize one of my kids being severely ill.

Basil was the VP of Procurement at this company. Basil was a class act. When I was negotiating deals with Basil, he would push you to the edge but was always aware enough to never push you off that cliff. Over dinner one night, Basil talked to me about his son who died of cancer. Both of us openly shed tears before the main course. My heart broke in a million pieces.

Valerie was a multi-talented administrative assistant who I worked with at this company. Whenever I would come to her location, I would always make it a point to grab coffee with her. I wanted to thank her for all her help.

One time we were grabbing a coffee in the cafeteria and somehow, she didn't look right to me. I asked her if everything was OK. She said it was. Yet something seemed off. I asked her a couple of more times and she just shrugged it off. Then it hit me. Her hair was crooked. Valerie told me that she had recently had chemotherapy and was wearing a wig. My heart broke yet again.

A few weeks later, I called Logan, Basil, and a few of our friends. We hatched a plan to raise money for kids with cancer. We would shave our heads to raise money for St. Baldrick's foundation and support a cause that meant a lot to us.

Over a period of three months, we cajoled, prodded, and nudged everyone we knew to help make a difference. Both Microsoft and this pharmaceutical company came together for a common purpose and that's when we really started to know the heart and culture of both of our companies. We began to deeply care about the people we were working with.

The fundraising initiative brought out a sense of fun and community. We gave out weekly prizes, I dyed my hair a different color and we even promised to have Logan teach bacon frying and grilling lessons for free!

Sometimes you hear a calling. It starts small and soft. Then it slowly picks up and the beat gets stronger and faster. It then echoes into a crescendo that you can no longer ignore. That's what our fundraising for St. Baldrick's felt like. The one universal thing that we can all agree on is that besides family and friends, our health, and that of our kids, is probably the most important thing to all of us.

Finally, on the designated day, we all shaved our heads. We couldn't believe the outpouring from both of our companies. In our first year, we raised over $30,000 for St. Baldrick's. In our second year, we raised over $50,000.

In the course of fundraising for this charity I got to meet a slew of folks at the customer company that I never would have met otherwise. The story of our fundraising campaign even got published in the local newspaper.

Logan, Basil and I were thankful that we were able to do a bit of good to recognize and support all of our friends and families who may be suffering from cancer and serious illness.

With the help of hindsight, I can honestly tell you that no amount of strategy, maneuvering, or planning could have helped me with this customer. Until I lived, breathed and bled their culture I was never going to break in. Does culture eat strategy for breakfast? I would say it does every time!

Is understanding your client's culture on your menu this morning?

Lessons Learned:

➢ Culture does eat strategy for breakfast. Most mergers and acquisitions fail because of people and cultural fit. History and industries are littered with these failures.

➢ When looking for a company to work for, really understand the company's culture and how it fits with you. A great company that is the wrong cultural fit for you ultimately leads to disaster.

➢ To be part of the fabric of a company, you really need to understand their culture and what makes them tick. That is the best long-term approach to building relationships.

➢ To be a well-rounded sales rep, you need to focus on other things besides the numbers. These include getting involved in the community, giving back and finding ways to make a difference. People want to know how much you care, not how much you know. Try to find a company that has a culture that supports this type of thinking.

➢ Be aware that company cultures change over time.

CHAPTER 9

Ebbs and Flows

I have this scene that is etched in my cerebral cortex. It's something that will always stay with me; the way it's hard to erase the memories of your first girlfriend, the first time you drove a car faster than you should, or the first time you beat all of your friends in full contact table tennis.

In *Shawshank Redemption,* Morgan Freeman stands in front of the parole board desperately trying to get early release for a crime he committed in his youth. He is showing remorse, saying all the right things, slicker than 10W30 full synthetic motor oil.

However, the board is still not buying it. Thirty years and countless appearances before the parole board, Morgan stops trying to schmooze his way through. In the end, he just tells them the truth. His one big regret is that he was so dumb in his youth. He did something horrible and wasn't aware enough to know the difference. It is this truth that finally gives him what he wants. Freedom!

To me, work-life balance is a lot like that conversation with the parole board. In my case, the parole board represents my wife. For the longest time I feigned regret, made promises that I knew I couldn't keep. I tried to sell my wife on my vision of the future. Make massive sacrifices now I said, work hard, save, and thirty years from now we would be set.

Then one day it hit me. Boom. I had bought into the whole work-life balance dream the way I had bought into the dream of being in the NBA at just 5'1". There is no such thing as work-life balance. There are just ebbs and flows. At certain points, your professional life is really important and you focus all your energies and time on that. At other times, your personal life is more important so you focus your time and energy on that. That's it.

My search for professional/personal harmony led me down the path of asking the wrong question. The question isn't, "What can I give up today to have what I want tomorrow?" The reality of life is that winning costs. It takes a tremendous amount of dedication and effort. The key question here is, "Are the intrinsic and extrinsic rewards worth the price you have to pay?" There is no right or wrong answer, just ebbs and flows.

Malcom Gladwell's <u>Outliers</u> and Geoff Colvin's <u>Talent is Overrated</u> are different riffs on the same theme. In theory, it takes approximately 10,000 hours of hard, dedicated practice to get to a level of expertise in any field. It takes the right focus, the right practice and most of all, commitment.

Cloud technology today is as ubiquitous as kids having cell phones. However, five years ago it was like the feeling shared by a new married couple. There was a lot of hope and promise but you weren't sure how it was going to play out.

Here's where it got really interesting. Try selling hope and promise to a highly-regulated global bank with massive footprints in Canada and the USA after the financial crisis of 2008. Selling ice to Eskimos in December would have been easier. That's the challenge we were up against.

I had just moved to Toronto from Chicago. I enjoyed working with my new customer. I was whipping my team into shape. I could now openly indulge in contraband (Cuban cigars). Life was good. God bless Canada!

Peter was the cloud specialist on my team. We were partners in every sense of the word. Together, we developed a sales strategy and campaign to sell cloud services to this financial services firm in Canada. Together we pushed the envelope and our teams to achieve the impossible.

For a period of a year, we gave the same presentations 100 times to the same customer. We had 200 detractors at our customer giving us 400 reasons why they would never buy cloud from Microsoft. On top of that, we had to deal with financial regulators who could straddle the fence better than Humpty Dumpty. It didn't matter; Peter and I were going to sell ice to Eskimos.

Slowly we started to chip away at the arguments and reasons why this customer couldn't go to the cloud with Microsoft. We helped build a business case and got stakeholder alignment. We got both of our legal and engineering teams to a place where they were uncomfortable but could live with their respective positions.

66

We were completely inseparable. We worked together 60-80 hours per week for over eight months straight. We saw each other more than we saw our families. We cancelled vacations, worked through weekends and were negotiating with legal teams at 11:30pm on Friday nights when all of our friends and co-workers were either still at the bar or in bed.

There was nothing we wouldn't sacrifice for this deal. We bled enough to meet the Red Cross goals for a whole year. We were completely committed to getting this deal done because it was the right thing for both companies.

Doing this deal took a massive personal toll on our whole team. Peter and I were just the tip of the spear. There were hundreds of our team members behind the scenes pulling all the strings and changing Microsoft to make this deal happen. Somewhere along the way, they all realized it was worth paying the price as well.

When Tim Robbins falls to his knees in the rain (in *Shawshank Redemption*) after breaking out of prison, we all cried. We felt his joy and pain at the same time. The universe was right again. Karma had found its way.

That's how Peter and I felt when we won the deal. This customer signed the biggest cloud deal for Microsoft in financial services history. There was no magic formula to winning. It just took a lot of hard work and commitment. Winning costs. The key question here is, "Are the intrinsic and extrinsic rewards worth the price you have to pay?" There is no right or wrong answer, just ebbs and flows.

Lessons Learned:

➢ Work-life balance is a myth, a unicorn at best. There are only ebbs and flows. At one point in time, your professional life may be very important so you focus on that. At other points, your personal life becomes the most important thing so you focus on that.

➢ Winning costs. It is just a matter of whether you are willing to pay the price for it, or not. There are no right or wrong answers to this.

➢ When the wall is falling all around you, take a breath, get a good night's sleep and start all over again the next day. It will always be better.

➢ Friends and co-workers matter. For anything significant and meaningful, you can't do it alone. You need a team of people behind you to do much of the heavy lifting that is required for great achievement.

➢ As much pressure as you feel in closing a deal, your customers experience the same, from their side. Know that you both have shared and common goals. That's why you are working around the clock together.

➤ Make sure you have back channels to remove roadblocks or log jams. In complex negotiations, there will be multiple times that you get stuck. The back channels will help break the log jam in a way that will help everyone save face.

➤ Celebrate the small victories along the way. It will help you get through the tough times. It is not just about one big event at the end.

➤ Selling a big complex deal is a marathon, not a sprint. Eat well, exercise and take care of your body because you need the energy to sustain yourself for the long haul.

➤ Thank everyone at the end and acknowledge their contributions. It took a village to get a big deal done. You didn't do it by yourself. It would not have been possible unless everyone contributed.

CHAPTER 10

They Call Me Bruce

It's funny how life never turns out the way you think it will. I was always a very small kid and not very strong. I think that's why I was so innately drawn to the martial arts. I knew deep down that I needed to learn how to defend and protect kids like myself. I wanted to defend the innocent from the bullies, tyrants and corrupt emperors of the schoolyard. Then one day I blinked and all of a sudden I was in my late thirties. A lifetime had passed, and I realized

I had never gotten into one fight. I don't even think I was ever in a situation where a fight would have broken out.

Like most Asian kids, I grew up idolizing Bruce Lee. Here was a guy who was charismatic, intelligent, and could whoop anyone's butt with just one finger. I watched all of his movies so many times that I perfected the menacing stare and ripping off my pajama top in that nonchalant way just to let you know that your day of reckoning was here. While other kids were fawning over Han Solo and Luke Skywalker, I was in love with the martial arts. It was good guys vs. bad guys. The good guys were always the underdogs who overcame insurmountable odds to beat the bad guys. They were noble in their quest for righteousness and were there to protect those who could not protect themselves. Martial arts was so simple and pure. You didn't need a lightsaber, an X-wing fighter, or a blaster to fight the bad guys. You just needed your hands and feet. Years of training under a master would ensure you had all the skills necessary to defeat any foe.

To an outsider, I lead a charmed life. I travel the world, live on the company's expense account, and the hardest thing I do every day is type on a keyboard. But this couldn't be further from the truth. I've been working 70-80 hours a week for over two decades now. Stress, pressure and the always-on world we live in today have taken their toll. While the kid in me was still worried about protecting everyone else from tyrants, I should have been thinking about how to protect myself from me. When you work as much as I do, you leave very little time to focus on your health, family or self. This is why I started taking karate.

The Sifu (Master) I faithfully followed in the movies as a kid is now Sensei Mike in the dojo. For the first time in my life, I was learning how to kick and punch the right way. Ichi, Ni, San... I started dreaming about karate the way Jiro dreams of sushi. I love karate because when I am in class, I have no choice but to focus. Without pure focus I will get hurt, or worse, hurt one of my classmates. This is therapeutic in so many ways because I have to mentally shut off everything else. At the end of the night, my classmates see me drenched in sweat. What they don't see is the stress and pressure washed away and beaten up by karate training.

I also love karate because it is clearly broken into stages. You can't run until you learn how to walk. The different belts and stages are a great checkpoint to take inventory of your skills and what you need to learn to progress to the next level. The journey and progression through the belts parallels my journey to becoming a better version of me. I am now in better health, more grounded in family and friends and have a better perspective on life.

Taking karate late in life has been a humbling experience. Your body doesn't do what you want it to and it doesn't bounce back as quickly as you would like it to. There is so much to learn. And just when you think you have mastered something, you realize that it was only the beginning. But just as in life, it's not about the destination (black belt), it's all about the journey and enjoying every stage that you are at. It's about learning and growing each step of the way to become a better version of yourself. I am so grateful for what karate has given me and plan to pay it forward. I am forever indebted. Domo arigato, Sensei Mike! Thank you for helping me to become a better version of me.

Lessons Learned:

- ➢ "Life moves pretty fast. If you don't stop and look around once in a while, you could miss it." – Ferris Bueller

- ➢ Star Wars does rock.

- ➢ Practice karate or other very strenuous physical activities in your teens or twenties. Doing it in your forties hurts too much!

- ➢ There is no shame in being beaten up by 14- and 16-year-olds.

- ➢ Martial arts will fundamentally change you. You stop being afraid. The only exception is that you may still be scared of your spouse!

- ➢ Never give up. In a period of four years I drenched the dojo with 982 liters of sweat, made 144 visits to the chiropractor and prayed 213 times to God that my teenage classmates don't beat me up too badly in sparring class. Yahoo! I finally got my black belt!

CHAPTER 11

The Challenger

The best sales reps I've ever met all shared some common traits. To be sure, they had different styles and approaches but their outcomes were always the same. They blew out their numbers and made a lot of money. They did it with unwavering conviction and faith. They did it with a passion that would rival Jesuit priests on a mission. They all believed they had the hardest job in the world.

For the longest time, I believed the same thing. The front-line sales reps were the most important people in any company. Without them, there would be no revenues. Without revenues, there would be no business. The rest of the organization - functional areas such as marketing, finance, HR, and operations - only existed to support the sales teams.

<u>The Challenger Sale</u> by Matthew Dixon and Brent Adamson is a great book that talks about the evolution of sales. Their studies show that the top performing reps in most corporations are the ones who challenge their customers by pushing the envelope on how to increase revenues or reduce operational costs. The best reps are the ones that teach, tailor, and take control.

This book is a lot like when some crazy Quebecers first started putting cheese curds on top of fries and then had the audacity to pour some hot gravy on top of it. Clearly they must have been drunk. It was so right and yet so wrong at the same time. I finally found my manifesto. I found a loving commanding officer who told me it was ok. It was ok to blow things up.

I was the Global Business Manager for a financial services company. Banking and commerce is as old as time. The VPs that I worked with were born in the 1960s and thought that Father Time had died of a heart attack because everything they did was frozen in time. Analytics, IoT or cloud computing, these might as well have been Martians or UFOs. They weren't buying any of it.

It didn't take me too long to figure out who was the dead wood and who was holding the company back from truly transforming into a digital retailer. A stick of dynamite here, a pack of C4 there. Boom Boom Pow. That wasn't just another Black Eyed Peas song. That was our sales strategy, and it worked.

In a short period of time, I became the most hated man at this account. I had enemy fire from every angle and every position. The customer executives were looking for a lynching and they were going to get theirs. Forget that "No Retreat, No Surrender" bullsh*t. It was time to go into hiding. I found a cave and laid low for a few weeks until the dust settled.

Brett - my mentor, my rabbi, and also the client's Global CIO - is a southern gentleman. He talks in a deliberate manner with a southern drawl that lures you into believing he's just another Forrest Gump. And that's when he gets you. Unbeknownst to everyone else he's got a PhD in common sense and insight.

When I finally came out of my cave, I made a beeline to Brett's office and asked for his help. I told him my woe is me story about how his SVPs and VPs were gunning for me. I was a marked man. I did my best *Jerry McGuire* imitation and told him to "help me help you." I sold it hard.

Brett knew my heart was in the right place and he was going to help. In that slow, deliberate way he told me he would provide the air cover I needed to survive, but that Microsoft was missing the mark. He said Microsoft didn't have all the answers. If Microsoft was going to break into financial services, we truly needed to help the banks figure out regulatory and compliance.

In that moment of clarity, Brett completely nailed it. <u>The Challenger Sale</u> talks about challenging your customers, but it is missing a chapter. You also have to challenge yourself. You have to look introspectively to see if you have pushed the boundaries of what can and should be done. You have to challenge yourself internally just as much as you challenge customers.

OMG. Let me say it out loud because three letters won't do it any justice. Oh My God! Selling internally is ten times harder than selling to customers. I had no idea.

Weeks turned into months and months turned into a year. Pushing the Microsoft legal and engineering teams and getting them to see the customer perspective so that we could move on our positions is like rolling a snowball uphill in the middle of July in Texas. It is not for the faint of heart.

As Microsoft was going through its transformation, our executive team had this great saying. "We are building the plane as we are flying it." Cognitively, everyone knew that was what we were going through. But the reality is that no one wants to be on that wing with you putting in the final rivets as you are 30,000 feet in the air.

After pissing off all my peers, colleagues and management team, I did the only thing you could do if you needed to hide out for a while and wanted to be completely untouchable. I hitched a ride with Elon Musk's Falcon 9 rocket and hung out at the International Space Station.

In that moment of darkness and quiet (and there was a lot of that in space), I realized how easy I had it. Selling to customers is easy. Selling internally in a large global matrixed organization is 100 times harder than anything I will do in external sales.

Lessons Learned:

- ➤ Sales reps by their very nature have an overinflated sense of self. The faster they realize this, the faster they will become better sales reps.

- ➤ In large, complex global organizations, selling internally is probably harder than selling to customers. There are so many constituents and stakeholders that if you don't get their support, situations can become very difficult very quickly.

- ➤ Don't be afraid to break the glass and challenge your customers. At the same time, be thoughtful of the glass you are breaking and its repercussions.

- ➤ Don't be afraid to challenge your own management and leadership team. I think this is where The Challenger Sale comes short. We have to have the internal fortitude to challenge ourselves just as much as we challenge our customers. It can't be a one-way street.

- ➤ Be respectful. You can challenge those around you but do it with respect. Good companies today will not condone bad or disrespectful behavior.

CHAPTER 12

What's Wrong with
Balanced Scorecards?

When I started working for this prestigious high-tech company, I was blessed. God reached down and tapped me on the shoulder. He gave me one of the best mentors to make sure that I would be successful.

John was a master. Everyone internally loved him. All of his customers loved him. He made so much money that

Warren Buffett would be jealous. John had been to President's Club more times than Anthony Bourdain has been in the kitchen.

After the first few weeks of orientation, John sat me down and told me the gospel. According to John, the key to survival at the company was to switch jobs every two years. Just play the metrics and that's how you make money. He said if you didn't like your manager, it didn't matter. They would be gone anyway. I took copious notes and outwardly thanked him for his wisdom.

What The Frank? God hadn't blessed me. He had forsaken me and instead was in line to get tickets to see *Star Wars - The Force Awakens* with everyone else. Didn't he know the lines were long? What kind of mentor tells you to play the system and just move every couple of years to find a new gig? What about making a difference? What about doing something great and transformative?

My nine-year-old daughter, Jahnis, came home crying one day. It turns out she had completely flunked her math test. What was puzzling to my wife and I was that Jahnis is a really bright girl. She's academically inclined and is a quick study.

As we dug into it, we found she had followed her teacher's instructions completely and fallen off the cliff. In school, they were teaching her how to fill in the bubbles as quickly as possible so that they could ace the mandatory standardized tests. They were studying to ace the test, not studying to actually know the material. These tests would then be used to grade the teachers, which in turn would be used as the basis for school funding for the next fiscal year.

We sat our daughter down and told her that she was approaching it completely the wrong way. We told her she should go back to the core skills and actually learn the math. We started using flash cards and implemented daily drills with her. We told her that once she got the math down, the speed would come.

As I got to know the company and my teammates, there was always talk about how the culture had changed. I had heard so many stories about "back in the day..." However, these weren't like the stories that your grandfather told you about how he had to walk two miles to get to school as a kid and that he walked uphill both ways. These stories were rich in comradery, esprit de corp and people doing the right things to make a difference.

No matter how many people I talked to, the answer was always the same. The company and culture had changed with the introduction of the scorecard system. I really didn't understand that at all. I had studied balanced scorecards in business school and knew that they were a good thing.

Balanced scorecards are a strategy performance management tool first used in the mid 1980s and then popularized by Robert Kaplan (Harvard Business School professor) in the early 1990s. Today over 90% of US companies use them and they are the most popular management tool for increasing performance.

Here's an example of a balanced scorecard.

Metric	YTD Forecast	FY Forecast
iPhone	●	○
Mac	●	●
iPod	●	●
Cloud	○	○
Customer Service	○	○
Break Fix	●	●
Consulting Services	●	●
Employee Engagement	○	○
Watch	●	●
TV	○	○
Customer Experience	●	●

The reason that balanced scorecards are effective is that they focus on Financial, Customer, Internal Business Processes, and Learning & Growth all in one pane of glass. It allows senior executives to use tangible metrics to support corporate strategy.

Balanced scorecards are a product of the 1980s. This was a time when we had real life Gordon Gekkos who triggered a wave of mergers and acquisitions. These M&A activities lead to huge conglomerates that had very diverse businesses all cobbled together. That lead to the creation of the Chief Operating Officer as the unifying force and balanced scorecards helped the COO evaluate strategies.

But are balanced scorecards applicable in the high-tech industry? One of the biggest criticisms of the balanced scorecard is that it doesn't take into account political or personal repercussions.

In high-tech, the pace of innovation and the speed at which companies change course lends itself to a change in strategy every one or two years. In that type of an environment, are balanced scorecards effective in managing output and productivity? Or do they create knee-jerk reactions that wreak havoc on culture and morale?

To me, balanced scorecards are a lot like the standardized tests that my daughter took. They are good in that they level the playing field and provide a consistent measure of what success looks like. They are bad in that they can be gamed. If all you focus on is getting the scorecard green (filling in the bubbles) and not focus on actually doing the <u>right</u> thing, it eventually catches up to you. That's when you have to pay the piper.

Lessons Learned:

➤ Metrics drive behavior. Make sure you have the right metrics in place to drive the behavior that you want to see.

➤ Balanced scorecards, like all other metrics, can be gamed. They are not infallible.

➤ Companies that over-index on one metric or system always end up having to compensate to overcome unwanted side effects.

➤ Focus on core skills. In high pressure situations, you always revert to the mean. And if you don't have core skills to fall back on, you might find yourself in a tough situation.

➤ There is no short cut to success. It just takes a lot of hard work. If you don't put in the time and effort, you will not build the muscle memory to be successful. Playing games and manipulating metrics is a short-term play. Focus on the long term.

Trong Nguyen

CHAPTER 13

Surviving with Chill Pills

It's so true what they say about your 40s: these are arguably the best years of your life. By now, most of us have gotten to certain points in our careers that we are happy with. We've made enough money where we are no longer living the student lifestyle. And our kids have started to sprout and grow into their own.

By now, we've also been battered and bruised by life. Whether it be in our personal or business life, we have all the battle scars to prove it. It's interesting to look around and see who is still standing and who has fallen down and can't get up.

I watched Leo DiCaprio in *The Revenant* and was as mesmerized as everyone else. You could feel his pain and knew what he was going through. We have all experienced some type of setback that made us want to suck our thumbs in a fetal position until the outer epidermis became irreparably damaged.

Laurence Gonzales wrote an inspiring book called Surviving Survival. I have it as a must read for my team. It talks about the art and science of resiliency. It gives some fascinating stories about people who have survived near-death experiences and shows why some people get through them while others succumb and give up. The insights and advice are just as applicable to our business life as they are to our personal life.

The type of customers that I work with are highly regulated, globally dispersed and have organizational charts that would confuse Data on *Star Trek*. The solutions that we sell at Microsoft are so complex (Cloud, Data, Analytics) that they essentially touch every aspect of an organization. As such, this creates the perfect storm. This lends itself to 12-18 month sales cycles for multi-million-dollar, multi-year deals.

I get asked a lot by sales reps what I think are the most important negotiation strategies when dealing with a complex global customer. Whether it is a combination of anchoring, give/gets, lead negotiator, etc., we all use the same strategies on the buy and sell side.

You can see a sample of some of the strategies we use in the chart below.

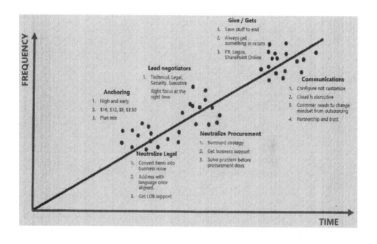

What I tell my team usually floors them. They were expecting some complex formula and calculated plan for how we were going to win the deal and become heroes in our company. What I tell them is, "Let's just survive it one day at a time."

The reality is, after a 12-18 month sales cycle, we'll have taken 100 twists and turns from our original plan. Deal fatigue sets in on both sides. Both companies want to get the deal done but there are just some minor items to deal with. If we had dealt with these items 12 months earlier, it would not have been an issue. But at the 11th hour, any issue that comes up always seems to be bigger than it really is. This is when surviving and resiliency means the difference between getting a deal done, or not.

I worked with a global financial services firm in Canada on a groundbreaking cloud computing deal where we would provide them with the capability to be agile and transform their company into a true digital bank.

Their lead negotiator, Catherine, was definitely one of the toughest negotiators I have ever worked with. Catherine has an infectious laugh and towers over most Smurfs at five feet tall. She is uniquely gifted at her job because she is blessed with two God-given talents. She can method act better than Al Pacino and she can teach Navy Seals how to creatively swear in a way that would make the toughest MMA fighters burn red with embarrassment.

Catherine and I were on a business trip in Seattle, WA. We had been in all-day sessions and we agreed that when we were done, we would go back to the hotel bar and continue our deal negotiations for a couple of hours before we reconvened with the rest of the team for dinner.

By now, we were two drinks into it, both of us exhausted from jet lag and lack of sleep for the last few days. We were both going pretty hard at each other. I don't recall what I said next but it completely set her off. "Trong, if you don't f**king give us these f**king concessions before the end of this f**king trip, I will kill this f**king deal. And I want deeper f**king discounts and I want another f**king drink now…"

"Sir, yes, sir!" I felt like one of the recruits in *Full Metal Jacket*. I cringed like any sensible person in that situation would. Deep down I knew this was a critical juncture in our negotiations and the key would be to just survive the moment and the day. With rest and a fresh set of eyes, we would both look at this differently.

So I said with the gravity and conviction of a priest at Sunday Mass, "Catherine, I know what we need to fix the situation. We need some of these." I opened my computer case and pulled out a bag called "Chill Pills." These were peanut M&M's that my son had given me.

Catherine laughed hysterically and we both survived the moment. We had many more of these moments as we got to the final steps of closing the deal. Each time a critical situation came up, my team and I took the same approach. Deal with the issue and survive it one day at a time.

Lessons Learned:

➢ Putting a plan together is always a good thing, but as you start to execute it, be flexible enough to change your course multiple times to find the right path. Contract negotiations are not a static thing.

➢ When you are in intense negotiations, always look for a way to break the log jam and lighten the situation. A bit of laughter goes a long way. Be prepared for complex negotiations to break down multiple times before they get back on track.

➢ Know who you are negotiating with and what makes them tick. Then use different negotiation techniques to get to the end result you want.

➢ Anchor early and make sure you have a detailed list of give/gets.

➢ Know the formal and informal people you need to influence to get a deal done. Make sure you know who your constituents are.

➢ Don't forget this is a mutual relationship. Customers need to close a deal just as much as you need to close a deal. Customers are geared toward getting things done just as much as sales reps are paid for selling things.

Trong Nguyen

.

CHAPTER 14

Sales Tips for New Sales Reps

People who are trying to break into high-tech sales often ask me what they should do to be successful. There are definitely some nuances to high-tech sales that no one thinks about before the issues arise, but in general I would tell them that sales is sales. The principles and foundations are the same across the board. In that way, you should be able to apply these fundamentals to any industry around the world.

In high-tech sales, there are generally three brackets of customers. You'll always get your "oddballs" that don't fit into one or the other category. More on those later. Most of your customers will be one of these three types, based upon the size of their company and how much they can potentially spend with vendors:

1. Small Businesses: These are usually highly transactional. Lots of little sales. And there are hundreds of thousands of these customers everywhere, localized into specific areas for the most part. These can be mom-and-pop shops or small businesses of up to 500 employees or so.

2. Medium Businesses: These are businesses that may have branches or affiliates in different states/provinces. They range anywhere from 500-1000 employees.

3. Large Businesses: These are businesses that have a national, international or global presence. They have anywhere from 1000-10,000+ employees, or more.

For the most part, high-tech companies that hire new sales reps out of undergraduate or graduate schools hire reps to look after customers in small or medium-size businesses, depending on how much experience they may have. Once they have proven themselves over time and have developed the deep sales experience needed to be serious sales reps, they will be promoted to manage the more complex and larger customers.

For now, let's concentrate on that moment when you're straight out of school and have very little sales experience. Here's my advice for new sales reps just starting out in their careers (the stuff I wish I'd known):

1. **Get a mentor.** Every company has their own unique culture and way of doing things. Don't expect to fit in right off the street. It's really important early on to figure out your company's culture in order to lay a foundation for success. In most companies, there are written rules of how to do things and unwritten rules of how things are actually done. Take care, because they are not always the same. This is "in-house" knowledge that can only be attained through personal experience. That's why getting a great mentor, or a handful of mentors for different viewpoints, is so critical when you are starting your career. Don't be shy. When you ask for help, most people are more than willing to give you the benefit of their experience. So ask for it!

Trong Nguyen

2. **Know your products inside and out.** It's hard to sell if you don't know what you are selling. Some people go into sales believing that it's all about the schmoozing. And that couldn't be further from the truth. Customers want to know how much you know, and how much you care. The foundation of that starts with you knowing your products with great depth. Study them and learn them. Pretend that you are still back in school and study like it's time for finals. Your test in sales is a little different, but the concept is the same. In high-tech, the products are always changing. That means by definition, you are always studying. It requires a lot of commitment but when you study and know your products inside out, then you have a great foundation upon which to build.

3. **Learn your competitor's products.** This is a step that a lot of people miss. It's hard to differentiate yourself if you don't know how your products stack up against your competitors. You have a great product? Wonderful, but so does your competitor. How do you sell yours against theirs? With knowledge. Therefore, it is crucially important that you study your competitor's products. When customers ask you about them,

you will be fully prepared to counter any sales blockers that come up.

4. **Understand your customer's business.** The best reps that I have ever met all have exhibited the same traits. They are sponges and students of the game. They spend a lot of time studying their customers to know their customer's business inside out. Some even reach a level of excellence enabling them to make recommendations that change their customer's perspective. When you get to that level, you become a trusted advisor. There is so much available information (annual reports, 10Qs, analyst calls, etc.) that you can ramp up on any business fairly quickly. It just takes commitment to digest and analyze all of the information.

5. **Know your internal processes.** Every company has different processes for sales, finance, operations, and so forth. Learn how your company really operates. Understand how the sales process works from end to end. Once you sell something, what happens behind the scenes? How does the order get processed? How do customers get technical support? How long will it take to get to the customer? What if orders are wrong? How do you go about fixing it? How do customers pay

your company? How do the Accounts Receivable and Accounts Payable teams interact with each other? What are the follow-up mechanisms in your company to ensure the best customer experience possible? By the way, I haven't even scratched the surface of all the questions you'll need to know the answers to!

6. **Connect the dots.** This is probably one of the most critical skills that you will need as you advance your career. How do you connect the dots between what your company can offer and what the customer needs? Recognizing those patterns and the ability to rapidly connect the dots will help accelerate your success in sales.

7. **Socialize.** Be with your peers and other folks in your company as much as possible. When I started my career, I made it a point of being with my co-workers whenever I wasn't with customers. I was a complete sponge. That allowed me to quickly learn aspects of the company not directly related to my job. I was able to learn the formal and informal power structures and how things really got done. Socializing and being out with my team members at company functions allowed me to see how

people behaved in social settings. This skill proved invaluable as I progressed through my sales career.

8. **Show up.** Half the battle in sales is just showing up. Be with your customers as much as possible. I always treated 9am - 5pm as customer time. Walk the halls. It was always surprising how much information I got just from being there, or the opportunities that would pop up because I was with the customer and walking the halls. If you spend enough time with your customers on a daily basis, eventually you get to know all of their habits, patterns, and what they like/don't like. This information is invaluable as you start building relationships with them.

Lessons Learned:

➢ Get a mentor. Multiple mentors would be even better. Mentors provide you with the guidance and direction you need to accelerate your career.

➢ Don't be afraid to ask the dumb questions. The more questions you ask, the faster you will learn. When you are starting out in your career, be a sponge. Learn as much as you can as fast as you can.

➢ If you make a mistake, that's ok. Own up to it as quickly as possible, learn from it, and move on. Most managers know you will make mistakes and will help you through it.

➢ Learn your products, your competitor's products and know the competition inside out. Be the expert that everyone looks to for help and guidance.

➢ Study your customers so you know them like the back of your hand. Know what your customers do and how their business actually runs.

➢ Spend time with your colleagues, managers and extended teams in a social environment. That is just as important as doing your job well. Develop those relationships and nurture them so that they become a permanent part of your network for the long term.

➢ Work hard. Put the extra hours in. You are trying to establish yourself. Let everyone know you have a fire in the belly and will do what it takes to get the job done right.

➢ Be thoughtful. You will work with a very diverse group of people. Be conscious of their background, likes, dislikes, etc. This will demonstrate that even though you are starting out in your career, you have emotional quotient as well as intellectual quotient.

Trong Nguyen

CHAPTER 15

Sales Tips for Intermediate Sales Reps

Now that you, the sales rep, have been in the industry for a few years, I want to pivot toward advice and recommendations for the intermediate sales rep. Here are some suggestions I think would be useful for honing and perfecting your sales skills:

1. **Relationship Alignment:** At this stage, reps should be able to build relationship maps. This

means understanding who the key players are in their customer base and what resources are available at their company so you can map out which relationships drive success. Reps should use the Myers-Briggs personality analysis to determine who can influence whom. Another suggestion is to have executive sponsors within the account on both sides. This ensures that there is a path for escalation when something does go wrong, which happens more often than you might think!

2. **White Space Analysis:** Here sales reps should look at what market share they currently have within the account and quantify the true opportunity. Look at who your real competitors are and where the opportunities lie; and build a long-term plan to go after that market share.

3. **Competitive Analysis:** This is where you look at your key competitors and put together plans to go after their business. Yes, we always look for opportunities to take business from the other guy! Using Michael Porter's Five Forces framework for analysis could be helpful here. This is a "point in time" view and can definitely change over a period of a year or two, depending on how fast their industries change.

4. **Partners:** The intermediate seller should have a complement of partners that they can call on to help with projects, execution, and ongoing sales campaigns. Partners can be very helpful in providing complementary skills and resources as well as amplifying your scope and reach with customers.

5. **Customer View:** At this stage the sales reps should have a good understanding of their customer's environment and be able to make meaningful suggestions for change. Suggestions can include operational aspects such as increasing efficiency or lowering costs. If the seller has deep lines of business relationships, he/she can make helpful suggestions on how the customer can grow their business by increasing revenues in new or tangent markets. An outsider's perspective at this point is always interesting and helpful. They might see something you've missed.

6. **Internal View:** At this point the seller would also be versed in their own company's environment. Just like their customers, most companies can always run better. There are often opportunities for improving efficiencies. Here the seller can make suggestions on how their company can

improve itself to become more customer focused and customer obsessed. Being on the front lines, the sales rep is in the best position to recognize these opportunities and make these suggestions.

7. **Resources:** By now the seller should have a good understanding of their extended and virtual team. The seller should be able to determine all of their strengths and weaknesses and use them effectively within the customer's environment. Where there are gaps or non-alignment, the seller should look to augment or replace those resources as appropriate.

8. **Self-Awareness:** By now the seller should also have a good understanding of their own capabilities. As Clint Eastwood once said, "A man's got to know his limitations." Everyone has gaps and can improve in certain areas. It is important for the seller to understand what those gaps are and close them with people who are experts in those areas.

Lessons Learned:

➢ Sales reps at this skill level should be able to do some deep analyses. These include relationship maps, white space analysis, and competitive analysis. Doing the analysis takes time and effort. The best reps are willing to put in both.

➢ Have a big network of partners and use them effectively. They can amplify your message/strategy and extend your reach. Be open and transparent with your partners. Tell them where you are willing to partner together and where you won't. They will appreciate that honesty, as you will not be wasting their time.

➢ Be mindful of who you put on your team. They will have a big impact on customer relationships. Make sure you have the best of the best working with your clients.

➢ Start branching out in different parts of your company (finance, operations, marketing, HR) to understand the jobs that those people do in your company. It will make you more rounded in your understanding of how your company actually works.

➤ Keep on learning. If there are management or leadership courses you can take to develop and hone your skills, be the first one to sign up.

➤ Be open to change. The high-tech world is always changing. If your company changes course, be open to change with it.

➤ Look for more mentors. Be intellectually honest and determine which gaps you still need to fill and find the right group of mentors to help fill those gaps.

➤ Mentor a new hire in the company. By now you will have enough experience to be helpful to new hires into the company. This will prove to be a great learning experience for both of you.

CHAPTER 16

Sales Tips for Expert Sales Reps

Here are the top sales tips for advanced sales reps:

1. **None of My Business:** In most large organizations, organizational distance between the top executives and the lowest salesperson can be five to seven levels of management or more! As a result, messages often get filtered or diluted; so when they do get to the top, what appears to be the "right" course of action can be very different than

what it should be. As advanced sellers, it is imperative that we provide as much straight talk to the executives as possible concerning our activities. They may or may not agree with our point of view but at least they will have more data points to make decisions. In my experience, most of the executives I have worked with have always found this sort of communication a breath of fresh air. Too many times sales reps just tell them what they want to hear as opposed to providing them with real, tangible facts. Stop being afraid of your boss. Be respectful, be a good employee, but give them the truth!

2. **Complementing the Leadership Team:** At this point, you should know the leadership team inside and out. You should know their strengths and weaknesses. You should know the direction in which they want to take their teams and what it will take to get there. This is where you can add the most value. Your industry connections and the senior executives you have met along the way may be able to help the leadership team at your customers. This is where you can connect the dots from some of the top execs in your rolodex to your customers, to make the best sales possible. As with

all executives, yours are on the lookout for top talent to augment their teams. Companies such as IBM, McKinsey and Accenture are really good at this. Their Client Partners are wired to provide this level of guidance to their clients, and it works.

3. **Marketing:** As sales people, we often think that it starts and ends with us. In reality, that is not the case at all. We are just one pillar supporting the overall business machine. The best sellers know this and figure out how to use the other pillars in business to forward their agenda and help their clients. One of these pillars is marketing. We need to consider both internal and external perspectives. Internally, the seller should work closely with their marketing teams to ensure that their clients know about and are well represented at all of the key marketing functions that their company will have over the course of the year. This should happen in all of the major cities where the client operates. The next level would be to get the marketing teams from the customer to work with your marketing team to come up with joint marketing ideas. Done right, you will have effectively found different ways to help your customers grow the revenue side of

their ledger. Now you have affected their business in a meaningful way. Imagine their gratitude!

4. **Partners:** The issue with most technology providers is that they provide a niche product or are a part of a small ecosystem in a sea of larger ecosystems that make up the fabric of their customer's environment. So the solutions they recommend (while good) may take a very myopic view of the world. This is easier said than done but if you can, zoom out a bit and really understand the complete ecosystem that will make the customer's environment work well. From there, you can recommend the best solution. This will result in you promoting your solution, but also understand that you may have to work with some of your competitors to provide the best end-to-end solution to your customer.

5. **Operations & Engineering:** Historically, the software industry has been characterized by hit-and-runs. You work really hard, sell your customer a software solution, they buy it, and then you run. The implementation and how it will work afterwards is someone else's problem. In the age of cloud solutions, this hit-and-run scenario doesn't really work anymore. Now when

customers buy solutions from you, they are essentially buying a service. You, as the provider, are responsible for the operations and running of the service. Now you are intrinsically tied at the hip. Your mutual success depends on the seller being able to help with the execution and ongoing operations of what you sold to the customer. This is why ensuring that your operations and engineering teams are tied closely to the customer's operations and engineering teams is so important. The two need to be in complete simpatico.

6. **Transition Plans and Succession Planning:** If you are looking after a large global customer, chances are you probably manage a team that spans anywhere from 20 to 100+ resources. The different resources on your team – from sales specialists, to customer service specialists, to project managers, and so on – are all at different stages in their career and different levels of customer interaction. It is really important to understand where everyone sits on this spectrum and plan accordingly for the next few years in terms of client transition and succession planning. This ensures that when the time does come to move resources in and out of the client business, there

will be minimal disruption. It is also important to plan your own succession planning. At a minimum, you should plan to stay with your customers for three years. The first year is really just a ramp up and learning year. The second year is when you start to make a real impact for your customers. The third year is when you have everything humming and running smoothly. There are always exceptions, but after years four and five there is a big potential for complacency and stagnation. Sometimes you just need someone new in the role to inject some fresh ideas, creative thinking, and a different outlook. Sometimes it takes something more.

Lessons Learned:

➤ At this stage, you should behave and act like a partner in a consulting firm. You have the depth and breadth of experience to make a difference within your own company and your client's. Be thoughtful of how you can help your company and your customers grow.

➤ Provide direct feedback and guidance to the top-level executives that you are dealing with at your customers. You will stand out because 90% of the time, they do not get this type of feedback from other sales reps.

➤ Use the marketing team to amplify and shape your marketing strategy with your customers. It will be invaluable to your success.

➤ As a Client Director or Global Account Manager, you are no longer just a sales rep. You have the ability to impact company directions and strategies. Take that responsibility seriously and act like the executive that you are.

➤ Trust your judgement. At this level, you will be bombarded with information and people will come at you from every angle with their own objectives and agendas. Filter it all and make sure you don't stray from your true north.

➢ Be humble. By now you are an expert in your field. That doesn't mean you stop learning. Be open to learning from all the people around you.

➢ Read more. Read anything and everything that you can get your hands on. The more knowledgeable you are in different topics, the more well-rounded you will be. The more well-rounded you are, the more valuable you will be to your company.

➢ Continue to network. Make sure your network is big and broad because you never know when and where you will need it.

➢ Just when you think you have everything under control, your world can easily turn upside down. Be ready for change!

CHAPTER 17

Getting Capped – Part I

Psychologists have done studies and gathered evidence that show people can overcome adversity through chemical manipulation. There are actually over twenty types of natural endorphins, the chemicals your own body produces that make you feel happy and relieve stress.

For example, when you exercise, your body releases endorphins. Expressing gratitude is also another way you can overcome adversity. Those who are truly grateful for what they have, rather than pining for what they don't have, naturally produce a higher level of endorphins in their body. Learning something new also triggers your body to release natural endorphins, resulting in a better ability to deal with the stress of adversity.

Through the years, I've developed an elaborate coping mechanism to deal with adversity and I've had great success with it. What I do is focus on the things that give me the most joy. I exercise. I read. I cook. You can always tell when I'm stressed because I end up running for two hours, finishing a book, and cooking up a huge feast all in the same day!

When you talk to people who have had near-death experiences, they always tell you the same thing; it is a moment that they will never forget. Everything plays out for them in slow motion. They can tell you exactly how fast their heart was racing, the number of breaths they took, and how images from their childhood sprang to mind one after another.

In my opinion, being in sales is a lot like being in a war movie. You stay on the front lines long enough, you will eventually get shot. It doesn't really matter what the reason is (politics, quotas and attainment, bad boss, new leadership, etc.). My heroes have always been the ones that get shot, bandage themselves up, and live to fight another day. War and sales. Like two sides of a coin.

My true love, though, is mobster movies. Whether it is *The Sopranos*, *Goodfellas*, or *Casino*, it always happens the same way. Out of the blue, you get a call from the boss or one of his lieutenants and they want you to go for a ride. You get in a car, everyone's being purposely vague about where they are going, and you drive to some place in the middle of nowhere. Then, bang! The hero is dead. Fun to watch. Not so fun to experience it first-hand!

I remember being shot like it was yesterday. It was just like in the movies. My manager pinged me out of the blue and asked to meet in a specific conference room. Then, as I walked down the stairs, my spider senses started to tingle. I knew it was going to be bad. I just had no idea how bad. Turning the corner to the conference room, everything started to slow down. In that split second, I realized I'd just taken that drive. The one where you don't come back. My heart was racing. I could feel every breath.

And then there I was, standing in an empty field. **Bang!** I was capped.

Lessons Learned:

➢ Losing your job is a devastating experience. It is ego crushing because our identities are so intimately and intricately associated with our jobs. Often, our jobs define us. Once you realize that the only thing that really got hurt is your ego, it allows you to move on fairly quickly.

➢ There are many lucrative opportunities out there. Don't be so set or stuck in your ways that you have to get a certain job or work for a specific company. Don't limit yourself. Be open to change.

➢ Embrace your loss, grieve, and then move on as quickly as possible. The longer you wallow in self-pity, the deeper you will go into the valley of despair.

➢ There will be moments of darkness when you feel completely bummed out. That is normal and OK. Your family and friends will pick you up and get you through it.

➢ Find ways to release the natural endorphins you need to feel good. This can include exercise, learning new things, and doing things that give you internal joy.

➢ In times of need, you will know who your true friends are. They are the ones that call you back and help in any way possible. Sometimes, the people you thought were your friends end up not being so. This is a great moment of clarity.

➢ If you can, take some time off. Recharge the batteries and enjoy life a bit before you start your new journey. Come back with a fresh set of eyes and sense of purpose.

➢ Keep perspective. Stop thinking about it so much. It's only a job!

➢ When you are ready, put a plan together on what you want to do and where you want to do it. Jobs and careers are like fish in the sea. There are a million options. You just have to pick the right one for you.

Trong Nguyen

CHAPTER 18

Getting Capped – Part II

I was driving home, in a complete and total state of shock. Somewhere along the way I must have blanked out. Suddenly all I could hear was Taylor Swift blaring on the radio. I don't know who it is that upset her but she was going on and on about **NEVER EVER** getting back together with him. How apropos.

Whether in your personal or your professional life, whether it was you who did the breaking up or it was you who got dumped, the feelings are the same. Everyone goes through the same stages of grief and loss. I had just been rejected – fired – by a company that I deeply cared for. It felt like I had been kicked in the gut by a pair of size twelve Doc Martins. I couldn't breathe. I was crushed.

For four days, I was rolled up in a fetal position. I sucked my thumb so hard I was going to put the Gerber baby out of a job. I embraced my loss and wallowed in my predicament with a vengeance. Even Oprah couldn't make me feel better now! After the shock came the sadness. I was sad not because I had just lost a job. I was sad because so much of my identity had been tied to my job. Trong = Work.

I used to get 150 emails every day. That's no word of a lie. My days were back-to-back with important meetings. People depended on me for advice, direction and guidance. Then, overnight, it all disappeared. The only emails I got now were ones from Expedia Vacations and Groupon. Damn it. Now I couldn't afford either!

For high-performing, achievement-oriented individuals, this is the hardest thing to deal with. Regardless of your profession or your level of experience, your job is you and you are your job. Your identities are inextricably intertwined. Or so I thought.

I immediately reverted to chemical manipulation. Natural chemicals, mind you. I needed endorphins, and lots of them. I put together a regimen of workouts for every day. I started reading a new book. I practiced gratitude. Every day I wrote down a list of all the things I was thankful for. The painful hours turned into days. The days turned into weeks and before you knew it, my winter turned into spring. Things started to grow and blossom again. Out of the sadness came new life.

A good friend and mentor of mine in Atlanta gave me the best advice when I called him up with my "woe is me" story. He said, "Trong, jobs and companies are like any other relationship. When you break up with one, the best thing to do is start dating again!" He was so spot on. When I started "dating" again by talking to different companies just to see what was out there, I was amazed. There were tangent and parallel worlds and universes that I did not even know existed. Elon Musk would have been surprised! There were opportunities and possibilities I hadn't even seen. I felt like I had just won the jackpot. The hardest thing I was going to have to do was decide where I wanted to go!

Getting fired is a humbling and life changing experience. The only thing that gets hurt in the process is your ego.

Once you realize that, you can get over it fairly quickly. I dated and dated and dated. And before you knew it, I had three marriage proposals!

Lessons Learned:

➢ Company culture is just like everything else. It is organic and it changes. What may have been a great fit in the beginning may not be a good fit later on. It is useful to do a pulse check regularly to see if the company culture fits you and vice versa.

➢ Use your network. Call everyone you know and tell them what happened. Talking about a traumatic experience is therapeutic and will help you get over it more quickly. It's also very likely that someone knows someone or a company that is hiring. That's how you get your leads.

➢ Treat a job search like a real job. Establish a routine and put in a full day's work. Finding a job is like any other sales pursuit. Build a funnel. Qualify the leads. Qualify some more. Negotiate the terms and conditions. Close the deal.

➢ Exercise every day. It is good for you and will help you release stress and pressure.

➢ You can't make finding a job a 60 to 80 hour work week. There is too much emotional baggage that goes with it. Put in 40 hours a week and then shut it off.

➢ When you shut it off, make sure you have outlets that will get your mind off trying to find a job. This could be reading, learning, hobbies, cooking, or anything that will release natural endorphins and make you feel good.

➢ The only one who can tell you that you CAN'T is you. And you don't have to listen to yourself.

➢ Don't jump at the first offer that comes along. It is a natural instinct to want security. Wait for the best deal, offer, and company to come along. Make sure you find the company that best fits you.

➢ When you land your new job, if you can, take some time off before you start your journey. Before you know it, it will be crazy times again.

➢ Be thankful and thoughtful. There were numerous people who helped you along the way to get through the tough times. Thank them.

AFTERWORD

I just closed an incredible chapter in my sales career. Over the last seven years, Microsoft has been an amazing place to shape the future of technology for enterprise customers. I am grateful for the highly-talented teammates, extended team, and leadership figures who I've had a chance to work with. Microsoft is changing the world with cloud technology and I am thankful I had a hand in shaping it.

Look forward to my next book where you will meet new characters and read stories that will make you laugh and cry. Good selling!

Trong Nguyen

ACKNOWLEDGEMENTS

This book would not have been possible without the expert editing of Shany Biran, Cabrina Attal, Kathy Clolinger, and Shawn Wells. They sliced and diced numerous drafts to enable me to tell this story the right way. They ensured that it had enough fact, educational tidbits, and emotion to make the stories compelling.

Thank you, Pia Reyes, for the awesome book cover design and illustrations.

Thank you, Krishna Venkatamaran, for encouraging me to write and tell the stories that needed telling.

Thank you, Randy Richardson, for being my partner and wing man as we forever changed the health care industry in the USA and moved the largest health insurance company to the cloud.

Thank you to my close friends Claude Richard and Elvis Vincent for being with me on the journey to completely transform the global banking and financial services marketplace in Canada. The ripple effects are still being felt globally.

I would also like to thank all of my Microsoft friends and colleagues. They are the inspiration and real-life characters that you just read about. Without them, the stories would definitely not have been as entertaining.

Thanks also goes out to the awesome customers that I have had the chance to work with over the years. Without you there would have been nothing for me to do. Thank you!

Thanks for reading my first book! Please add a short review on Amazon and let me know what you think!

ABOUT THE AUTHOR

It's hard to win against someone who never gives up. Trong Nguyen never gives up. As a seasoned sales and marketing executive, Trong specializes in turning difficult customer situations around. Trong has a unique ability to apply economic and business theory to practical applications in real-world situations. Never shy, Trong will have a point of view just divergent enough to make a difference and turn lemons into lemonade.

Evidence of Trong's prolific successes includes countless competitive wins, raving customer testimonials and profound case studies that have been leveraged extensively by industry insiders.

Trong currently resides in Toronto and Chicago with his wife Natalie and their three rascal kids.

You can reach Trong at:
www.linkedin.com/in/megatrong

Made in the USA
Lexington, KY
23 April 2017